To Audrey,

Here's to winning "BIG" !

Best of luck.

Nancy J. Davis

POETRY

BY
NANCY J. DAVIS

RoseDog Books
PITTSBURGH, PENNSYLVANIA 15222

RoseDog Books
701 Smithfield Street
Pittsburgh, PA 15222
Visit our website at www.rosedogbookstore.com

ISBN: 978-1-4809-6169-2
eISBN: 978-1-4809-6146-3

THIS BOOK IS DEDICATED TO

Tony Nicolette
Tom Caljouw
Libbi Caljouw-Alcock
Monica Clemente
Dave Davis
Bob Davis
Deanna Marleau
John Davis

And in Memory of my young brother

Chuck Davis

Order of Poems

I'm Walking My Dog

It's winter ... it's cold ... and I feel so darned old
As I'm **walking my dog** in the snow
The wind has a bite as we trudge through the night
With the temperature 13 below

The snow blinds my eyes ... My feet pinch with cold
As we head through a field in the storm
If it wasn't for him I'd be sitting in front of a fire
Where it's cozy and warm

With lips and cheeks frozen... I manage a smile
As I'm covered in white head to toe
A question in mind keeps repeating itself
"Just **who's** walking **who** in the snow?"

It's been just an hour ... but seems like a week
As my legs are beginning to freeze
What I wouldn't give for some warm summer sunshine
Instead of snow up past my knees

His bark breaks the silence ... he sees the porch light
But the snow is so deep he can't run
And I laugh as reality suddenly hits me
"This dog is just plain having fun!"

He races me home ... though he's awkward at best
He jumps high through the un-trodden snow
When he reaches the gate he's content to just wait
For this old man who's always so slow

Now the fire is crackling ... we both settle down
And relax in the warmth of its glow
But tomorrow you'll find me no matter how cold
I'll be **walking my dog** in the snow

In The Rain

In the rain an old man struggles
Just to walk along the street
His cane ... a constant saviour
Holds him steady on his feet

I watch and wonder sadly
How he ever got that way
He is dressed in ragged clothing
His long beard a matted grey

A red light stops his journey
So he rests for just a time
With a hill ahead… I wonder
"Will he ever make the climb?"

Melancholy takes control
I'm steadfast in my stare
With the question ever present
"Does the world around him care?"

Succumbed to his misfortune
He just stands there **in the rain**
And waits with calm endurance
For the green light once again

Poofy The Duck

Poofy the Duck would dawdle everywhere that he would go
And the other ducks would laugh at him 'cause he always swam so slow

His pond was very beautiful, surrounded by a park
Yet Poofy's favourite thing to do was swim alone at dark

Now Poofy's mother, Wanda, was quite worried for her son
So she saw the wise duck, Morton, just to ask what could be done

The wise old duck was resting but seemed glad that Wanda came
And when she told him about Poofy, he replied..."*Just change his name* !"

"*Oh my!*" she softly questioned... "*So that's why Poofy's shy*?"
Morton shook his head and answered... "*Yes, Wanda, that is why* !"

So Wanda sat and pondered. She thought about a name.
For days and weeks she struggled and one day it finally came

She rushed to look for Poofy to surprise him with the news
And she found him sitting all alone while others swam in "twos"

"*Poofy* !" Wanda called out loud. He slowly swam her way.
"*I've got great news to tell you*" and she changed his life that day

Poofy laughed and swiftly dived about when he heard his great new name
He would no longer play alone or hang his head in shame

"*So ... a name CAN make a difference*" Wanda sighed with such regret
As Poofy raced to spread the news. His new name was simply... **JET**

RAGS TO RICHES

From **rags to riches** I did go
Though costly it did seem
For old friends did desert me
As I chased my wildest dream

I climbed the ladder of success
Though fell from time to time
Yet nothing could impede my steps
As upward I did climb

And at the top I realized
It was really not that hard
For success cannot be measured
By an inch, a foot or yard

So ... if you would take direction
From this "old girl" past her prime
Chase your hopes and chase your dreams
It's really worth the climb !

Dad's Grandfather Clock

Dad's grandfather clock
Goes tick and goes tock
As it stands with its face a bit rusty
All night and all day
It keeps ticking away
And mom wipes it with socks when it's dusty

The pendulum swings
In constant display
With a squeak that sounds just like a mouse
Every hour it chimes
With a sound overwhelming
I'm sure that it shakes the whole house

It's been there forever
That grandfather clock
And I spy as dad watches in wonder
With a smile on his face
He waits for the moment
The clock strikes the hour … much like "thunder"

Well, I finally grew up
And moved out on my own
So my dad gave me something to keep
His old grandfather clock
That goes tick and goes tock
He said… **"Now I can get me some sleep** !"

Seasons

SPRING wakes up the flowers
From their long and wint'ry sleep
And when **SUMMER** is upon us
Love and flowers seem to meet

Their petals get all broken
As the **AUTUMN** brings the rain
And with **WINTER'S** cold white blanket
Until **SPRING** … they sleep again.

September 11th, 2001
(New York City)

A day in September… a typical morn
Millions starting their day
Others just being born

The New York skyline … renowned for its spell
Was about to be changed
By a terrorist "cell"

Some heard the plane coming … but paid it no mind
That was a mistake
The "unfathomable" kind

I was numb in my stare as it hit Tower 1
And the chaos that followed
Was second to none

Just off in the distance a second plane flew
It crashed with a vengeance
And hit Tower 2

The moments that followed were straight out of Hell
"***We're under attack** !*"
I heard someone yell

The Twin Towers crumbled and thousands were dead
Yet united we stood
For what else lie ahead

I was lucky, just barely, to live through the day
I was injured and bloody
When pulled from the fray

September 11th, 2001
A day the world witnessed
What "evil" had done

The Old Man By The Sea

An old man walks along the shore
On a dark and gloomy day
He holds a long and crooked stick
To help him on his way

I watch and paint with gentle stroke
And add him to my scene
I cannot help but wonder
Why he's there and where he's been

The clouds are black and threaten rain
As waves crash to the shore
Yet he sits alone with nature's wrath
As if to beg for more

I cannot paint another stroke
The wind … too much for me
So I bid farewell in silence
To **the old man by the sea**

The Lottery

I grab my coffee, toast and jam
I slept in late again
Jump in the shower, make it cold
Gotta wake my tired brain

My hum drum days all circle 'round
A job that pays the rent
On Mondays I just cry the blues
'Cause the weekend's come and went

My job's real tough and time goes slow
But when the work day ends
I go to dinner, drink some beer
And play cards with my friends

My car's a wreck, needs lots of work
Don't think it's gonna last
And all the kids just laugh and shout
Whenever I drive past

Girlfriends?   Sure !   I've had a few
There was Joan and Pam and Gin
But girls don't stay once they find out
My wallet's pretty thin

BUT … I might win **The Lottery**… a million bucks or so !
When that day comes
I'll quit my job
And tell them ALL just where to go   !!

A Horse Called Jack

My friend Willy has a horse in his field
And his name is Jack ... just Jack

He runs and enjoys the sun all day
With no one on his back

One day Willy said "C'mon Luke"
So up in the saddle I went

Jack didn't mind. He just turned and looked
But he seemed to be content

Jack started walking so I held on tight
It was time to learn to ride

I didn't have a clue where we would go
So I let Jack be the guide

"Wow ! This is fun ! I'm up so high
I can see the world from here."

And as Jack sped up and began to trot
I was brave and showed no fear

Willy gave a "whistle" and then Jack turned 'round.
It was time to head on back

But I won't forget my first time riding
On **A Horse Called Jack** ... just Jack

A Cup of "Latte"

Friends get together
In all kinds of weather
No matter what time of the day
They talk about family, jobs or whatever
While sipping **A Cup of "Latte"**

From Monday to Friday
They seem satisfied
With a regular workplace routine
When it's time for a break
They rush for Pete's sake
For their next great big jolt of caffeine

The weekends of course
Are a whirlwind of errands
For home and the kids and the critters
But when that's all done
You can watch them all run
To Starbuck's for more of the "jitters"

It's quite a big fad
In this world of high tech
To sit and enjoy a "latte"
And you'll find it won't end
It's a heck of a trend
"Cause it "blends" in with work or with play.

Numbers

Numbers are important as we live from day to day
The clock tells us it's time to leave and how long we can stay

When I'm driving in my car I always check the speed
And all the pages of my books are numbered as I read

When I was very young I learned that one and one are two
But **numbers** got much larger as through life I grew and grew

In sports we'd never realize if our team had won or lost
If we didn't count the **numbers** keeping score at any cost

I wanted to be 20 when I was only 10
And now that I am 40, twenty's come and gone "again"

Throughout our lives we celebrate with "countless" reasons why
And we dream of having "millions" once our youth has passed us by

So in summation of this poem I'll give you some advice
Count your blessings once a day or maybe even "twice"

Here's to Marilyn Monroe

Here's to Marilyn Monroe who I'm sure you all know
Was an actress men couldn't refuse
Still her mem'ry remains and her movies play on
After late night T.V. news

Her sultry blonde looks were second to none
And are still imitated in vain
Yet beneath her charisma and gleaming white smile
Was a heart that was so filled with pain

"Did she ever find true love?" She came close it's told
With a great baseball legend named "Joe"
He was quite the big "hit" with the ladies back then
And especially our Miss Monroe

Her death came quite suddenly... while she was young
I for one shed a river of tears
And like *Elvis* and *Bogart, Sinatra* and *Wayne*
Her legend has outlived her years

So as Hollywood's blonde lovely actresses
All try to turn history's page
Even though some are great, they'll still just have to wait
'Cause Marilyn's STILL ON THE STAGE !

Happy to be Free

A tiny bird was sitting on a branch atop a tree
He was singing and enjoying life … so **Happy to be Free**

His friend the large bald Eagle swooped down to get a glance
He stopped by, just to talk awhile, beside him on his branch

The tiny bird stopped singing and they both enjoyed the view
But soon the Eagle saw his prey so off again he flew

A little while went by and then a Crow dropped by to sit
The tiny bird stopped singing and, once again, he talked a bit

Now this went on for hours and though the company was good
The tiny bird just wanted to keep singing… if he could

He flew upon a house-top just to sing a song or two
But a friendly Sparrow joined him… not for long … then off he flew

A big black cat climbed up and scared the tiny bird to flight
He escaped into a tree close by where he could spend the night

Now the tiny bird is safe … where he cannot be seen
He blends himself among the leaves … the tree's thick leaves of green

Though darkness now surrounds him, he is **Happy to be Free**
And tomorrow you'll find him singing on a branch atop a tree

Today I Still Love You

Today I Still Love You
Though my mind and body weak
And the warmth of youthful passion
Remains constant as we speak

Our love was once a mountain
That we climbed right to the top
And the songs we sang so beautifully
Just never seemed to stop

Today I wisely speak these words
For tomorrow is unknown
And our yesterdays together
Like our dreams, have quickly flown

Through grateful tears I thank you
For all of our todays
Supporting me and loving me
In all your special ways

Our story will soon end my love
As all great stories do
Yet I have no regrets ….*not one*
Of all my yesterdays with you

Your Wedding Day

I cannot tell you sweet daughter of mine
What **Your Wedding Day** means to me
No words can express what I feel in my heart
Of this treasure God gave to me

As you stand in white lace with your man by your side
You are perfect as perfect can be
As he gives you his hand and you smile at his touch
Your love is for all here to see

The wedding vows start. It's the moment of truth
And your love has stood up to the test
You've become man and wife. What a beautiful day !
I know that your lives will be blessed

I'll cherish the years and mem'ries we've shared
For they're etched in my heart just like stone
And it's my greatest wish that the future will bring
A daughter like you… for your own.

The Rooster

When the sun comes up
The Rooster knows
'Cause cock-a-doodle-doo
He goes … He goes

All the chickens swoon
When they hear his call
'Cause they all love
This Rooster tall

The pigs go "Oink"
And the cows go "Moo"
When **The Rooster** goes
Cock-a-doodle-doo

And old farmer John
Jumps right out of bed
When he hears that sound
Ringing in his head

Cock-a-doodle-doo
Cock-a-doodle-doo
If you listen hard enough
You can hear it too !

My Cherry Tree

My Cherry Tree in spring does bloom
As I gaze upon it from my room
It's blossoms dance in the fresh sea air
And demand attention as I stare
The tree will soon have leaves of green
And cherries will complete the scene
I'll pick the cherries one by one
And when the tree is empty... I'll be done
When the summer sun shines down on me
I enjoy the shade beneath my tree
But when fall and winter show their scorn
My Cherry Tree looks so forlorn
With leaves all gone and branches bare
It's beauty will return next year

You're No Tiger Woods

There's the golf course yes indeed
Miles of grass without a weed
Beckoning to all who play
"Pay the price.   I'll make your day"

With fairways manicured they bring
A challenge with each club you swing
The greens...perfection as you putt
Ooooh... missed again !   You're in a rut !

Play 18 holes most in the rough
The "cuss" words flow.   This game is tough !
The sand traps all get in the way
And you lose more balls than you care to say

So, the golf game ends and your feet are sore
You're feelin' down but ...hey...check that score !
90 !   Wow !   That's the best so far
That's easy to beat with just one more par

Back to the pro shop to add your name
And reserve a time for your next big game
Sure.   You'll be back.   You're really hooked !
You've got the "bug" and your goose? ... IT'S COOKED !

You're No Tiger Woods with a caddy and fame
You only get that once you've "mastered" the game
And, oh yes... the word players often ignore?
It's a four letter word... *much like "GOLF"...* it's called ... FORE !!

Flowers

Flowers are an earthly treasure
As they dance upon the wind
You can find them everywhere you look
"Outside" and even "In"

Their beauty cannot be denied
You smile at just one glance
And through the ages they complete
The setting for romance

Thanks goodness for the flowers
As their fragrance fills the air
I just cannot imagine life
Without the flowers there !

Whiskers

The lightning scared me late last night
So I quickly ran to hide
My closet is my favourite place
It seems quite safe inside

I curled up in a corner
With a pillow for my head
My little cat called **Whiskers**
Came to share my "closet bed"

I shut the door behind him
And we snuggled up in fright
Soon sleep came to our rescue
And we made it through the night

Early in the morning
Still all snuggled up so warm
We listened for the thunder
And the lightning from the storm

*"It's gone !   We made it **Whiskers***
We no longer have to hide
The storm has turned to sunshine
And now we can play outside !"

I opened wide my closet door
Holding Whiskers oh so tight
Feeling happy that we both felt safe
In my "closet bed" last night

The Flight of John F. Kennedy, Jr.

A plane went down with 3 on board
...Carolyn, Lauren and John
Fate played it's hand and once again
Another "Kennedy" was gone

The days went on and hope had dimmed
Would the plane be found at all ?
In the waters off Cape Cod they searched
Where the plane had made it's fall

The three were found in their ocean grave
Which alone was a relief
"An American son has gone to rest."
President Clinton spoke in grief

John Jr. was the pilot
When the plane fell from the sky
And in history books it will be told
They were all too young to die

The country suffered, not just some
Throughout this whole ordeal
And to the Kennedy family ... once again
Their pain and loss was real

John was the *Prince of Camelot*
When they died in '99
And this tragedy will linger on
In the hearts of yours and mine

The Camel

The **Camel** is an animal who lives upon the sand
He is King of all the desert, loved by all throughout the land

He drinks a lot of water and he stores it up inside
So he can go for days without it in his travels far and wide

Sometimes he kneels and tucks his legs 'neath his large and hairy chest
And longs for the stillness of desert nights … a time that he likes best

He makes his presence noticed with his loud obnoxious bray
As he walks along the sun-baked sand in his world so far away

Like a Lion with *his* Kingdom… so the **Camel** has *his* throne
And it's there among the sand dunes that he truly stands alone

Yes… the world is full of animals, some strong, some mean, some weak
Yet the **Camel** rules unchallenged in his land of sand and Sheik

My Fridge

My fridge keeps the food nice and cold and so fresh
No matter what time of the day
If I'm stuck at the office or snuggled in bed
My fridge just keeps humming away

They come in all colours to suit each decor
In stainless steel, black, white or wood
And the ice-maker adds an incredible touch
As it crushes and cubes really good !

But the freezer … now that's just amazing for sure
I can fill it with pizzas and more
When the kids come home hungry from soccer or school
It's like having my very own store

And when friends just pop in for a coffee or snack
I can show them I'm quite a good host
"Cause **My Fridge** is like family … constantly there …
Just when I need it the most !

I Still Smell The Roses

The roses grow wild in the fields of green
As I pass them by on my cycling machine
The sun shines down from a sky of deep blue
And my eyes fill with tears ... I'm reminded of you

We rode together, just you and I
When we were young and our spirits high
Through spring, fall and the long winter too
I loved no one else, only you... just you

I miss you and do long to hold you again
Though I never will, time does lessen the pain
I Still Smell The Roses this beautiful day
With you here beside me... *a memory away*

At The Zoo

Mr. Monkey ... Mr. Monkey ... How are you today
I watch you swing from branch to branch and chatter as you play

Oh yes ... and there is Miss Giraffe standing up so tall
She looks at me when I pass by and wow I feel so small !

I love to watch the bears come out and frolic in their pool
The sunshine is quite hot today and that's how they stay cool

And look at Mr. Peacock with his feathers all fanned out
His colours are so beautiful of that there is no doubt

I love the Zoo with animals that come from far away
I wouldn't get to see them if they weren't here on display

Some of them are wild I know and some of them are tame
But I don't feel at all afraid ... I think they're glad I came

When I stare at them up close and they stare back at me
I wish that they could talk out loud and tell me what they see

It's time to go ... but I'll be back ... I love it **At The Zoo**
'Cause I get to watch the animals play ... *just like me and you*

26

The Good Life

Twenty years in school ... a lifetime to some
I struggled to have **The Good Life**
With no turning back I gave it my all
Couldn't settle to be *"someone's wife"*

My friends all got married when they were so young
They abandoned their hopes and their dreams
Some got divorced ... at least that's what I heard
Life didn't turn out well it seems

I kept myself focused though lonely at times
And I've just met a wonderful man
In the springtime of life things are going okay
It's all gone according to plan

"You can't have it all !" so I've heard it said
If you think *that* way it will come true
But here I now sit in my company Jet
Flying home where my problems are few

I made it !   I'm here !   I've worked hard for it all
And I'm blessed in such positive ways
I charted my course and I weathered the storms
Not bad for a woman these days !

This Mother's Wish

I remember it like it was yesterday ....

You stood by the door with your duffel bag at your side
And, if I could describe with *one word* how I felt at that moment,
It would have to be ... "**proud**"

You were my only son and we were a hug away from saying *"goodbye"*
I knew the day would come, but, how could I have ever known the reason why

Ever since you were a small boy you wanted to be a pilot... and ...
When you enlisted in the Air Force, your dream came true
The world has changed since you were that little boy
And it takes brave men and women like you to protect what freedoms we have left...
Wars are no longer far away
They are knocking on all the doors of the free world ... *and that must change* !

The day I got the telegram..............

I sat, holding it for hours, with tear stained eyes
Feeling the loss, pain and emptiness
Like so many mothers before me

How does any mother accept the death of her child !
There are no words to describe such grief

And now that you are laid to rest my son
It is **This Mother's Wish** that someday the world will be free ...
Free of the pain and suffering brought about by war
Only then will I know you did not die in vain
Only then could I possibly come to grips with your loss
And ... only then ... could I truly embrace and accept a reason
For which you so bravely gave up your life

28

A Son's Prayer

My heart cries out in silent prayer
As your loss I comprehend
And the memories will comfort me
As my heart takes time to mend
Profoundly ... and yet simply mom
When each new day is done
I will thank the Lord for knowing you
Especially ...   as your son

The Snowman

They started with huge balls of snow then a small one for my head
They smoothed me over with their hands
"Looks great !" the big man said
They made me tall … at least 8 feet … then got a ladder out
Two ears were placed upon my head
So I could hear them laugh and shout
A hug of warmth went through me as the little boy named "Bill"
Put his arms around me and took away the chill
I had black feathers for my hair, a carrot for my nose
Red jelly beans framed out a mouth … though gone were half of those
Then eyes of beets were placed just so and worked extremely well
But buttons made of brussel sprouts unfortunately fell
Around my waist went grandpa's belt … a little tight I'd say
And the big straw hat upon my head blew off three times that day
They placed a shovel in one arm, then gave me shoes for feet
Around my neck they wrapped a scarf … at last I was complete
So I stood there silent in the yard for many days and nights
How I loved to watch the children play when they had snowball fights
BUT … even though I'll melt away as the sun takes winter's chill
I won't forget the warmth I felt
From the hug of little "Bill"

Winter's Perfect Moment

The snow lies silent on the ground
Beneath the lamp post light
Twinkling like a million stars
In the gentleness of night
An old man in the distance
On a park bench settles down
For what seems a cold and lonely rest
From his journey into town
This is the best of winter
Silent … in the midst of night
No blowing winds or sleet or hail
Or clouds to hide moonlight
What beauty does life offer
To compare with such a scene ?
There is nothing comes to mind at all
At least not where I've been
There are no children playing now
No traffic noises blare
This is **Winter's Perfect Moment**
Seldom witnessed by my stare

Candles All Aglow

"Happy birthday gramps to you"
Their voices ringing clear
The time has gone by quickly
"Has it really been a year?"

The birthday cake is brilliant
With its **Candles All Aglow**
And the childrens' laughter bellows
As I cast a windy "blow"

I've had the best that life can give
As I reach 85
It's a life I treasure greatly
With each moment I'm alive

As all my children pamper me
With hugs and gifts galore
In the winter of my lifetime
Who could ever ask for more

It's the time of life for memories
And reflecting on the past
A time for simple pleasures
Making sure each one will last

So… At 85 and holding
As the celebration ends
I'll recall this day with fondness
Spent with family and friends

We Will Meet Again

I am alone with my mem'ries of you
"Why did it happen?"
A question I ask myself every day
Our life together was so meaningful
Blossoming into a wonderful future
A future that would still see us together
We would be weathered by the storms of time
Yet strong and alive in our hearts and minds
Satisfied with our long and treasured existence

As my life continues, I miss you more than words can say
Though new relationships have come my way
I realize no one else could ever take your place
I am still blinded by my love for you
Your memory is all I need to calm my troubled heart
I am sorry you missed your children in their successes
And watching your grandchildren laugh and play
They are so beautiful
They are so much like you

Even as I enter the winter of my life, I marvel at how much I still love you
After all these years
I am not the young woman you married … I am old
Yet at peace with who I am and what I have accomplished
Life has been kind and unkind, gentle and severe
Without you beside me I realized life must go on
I must be there for others for as long as I am needed

I take comfort in knowing … I did not give up
I take comfort in knowing … I gave my heart to the man I love
I take comfort in knowing that one day … **We Will Meet Again**

A Man Of Vision

You showed the world you were a leader
A fact not easy to ignore
You made mistakes ... to err is human
But so did men that came before

You gave your all to lead your country
In times of conflict you were "might"
And when confronted by your enemies
You showed them just how well you fight

With Yeltsin and Mandella
You saw that words were not in vain
And when you spoke, your allies listened
You were the anchor to the chain

You gained respect through strength and honor
And with countrymen did stand
With love and deep conviction
Of the United States ... your land

You proved the U.S. stands for freedom
And exemption from control
And as President ... was well aware
That freedom takes its toll

And on that note with soaring heart
We stand with heads raised high
And salute **a man of vision**
A friend of years gone by

This poem is dedicated to President Bill Clinton.... 42nd President of the United States.

He served from 1993 – 2001

My Dog Ralph

My dog Ralph loves to play outside
In the sun, in the rain, in the snow
He jumps so high to catch the ball
As I give it my best throw

When I whistle out loud he comes a runnin'
Can't wait to see what's up
A friend indeed, my dog called Ralph
I've raised him from a pup

On Saturdays we fish at dawn
He's patient just like me
Even though I seldom catch a fish
He loves my company

When I come home from school each day
He's waiting by the door
Now Ralph's a real big dog and when he welcomes me
I often wind up on the floor

When I do my homework in my room
He sprawls out by my chair
But as soon as I'm finished he jumps right up
Making sure I know he's there

You can have your cats and birds and fish
'Cause a dog can be a friend
And when life gets tough and it sometimes does
He'll be faithful to the end

Candlelight & Champagne

AS I ENTER THE ROOM ....

Your tanned and gorgeous body
Lies in wait upon the bed
Anxious for the passion
In the moments just ahead

I've prepared for this encounter
Like a fox to catch his prey
And as your eyes are fixed upon me
There are no words that I can say

The mood is set with candlelight
Soft music fills the air
The Champagne chilled and waiting
As our love we finally share

In that electrifying moment
When the earth does surely shake
The phone rings out like thunder
And from Heaven .... I AWAKE !

EVERY MOMENT

Is it when we lay awake and talk
And hold each other tight?

Or ... walk along the sandy shore
On a perfect moon lit night?

Perhaps it's when we're dancing
And you whisper in my ear

Or ... when I think of how we met
And fell in love last year

It could be in your absence
That I really feel your love

No ... It's **Every Moment** yet to come
And all of the above !

Mr. Snowy Owl

Mr. Snowy Owl in his feathers of white
Says "*Whooo Whooo*" on his branch at night

The wolves can hear and the bears can too
When **Mr. Snowy Owl** says "*Whooo Whooo*"

The animals feel safe and sleep so sound
'Cause they know at night Snowy Owl's around

He never seems to sleep.   He keeps watch 'till dawn
And when the animals awake … Snowy Owl is gone

So the animals play in the sun's bright light
In the rivers and the streams and it's quite a sight

The Eagle on his perch watches from up high
All the animals can see him as he soars on by

But when nightfall comes and makes the forest all black
Mr. Snowy Owl to his branch comes back

His eyes stay fixed on the ground below
Watching out for shadows that he doesn't know

Even though he's small he is very wise
As he sits there as a silhouette on moonlit skies

So … if you hear "*Whooo Whooo*" when it's late at night
You'll know it's Snowy Owl in his feathers of white

Legends have been written and I think it's true
Late at night Snowy Owl watches over you too !

A Child Of God

It's dark and cold here where I lay
In the silence of the ground
I can't reach out to hold you
Or talk with any sound
My heart no longer beats with life
Yet my spirit has great light
I am no longer visible
Each passing day or night
I was just 10 … **A Child Of God**
As all small children are
When a man came and took me far away
My life ended in his car
I recall that I was on my own
That warm October day
I didn't know that to play with him
Would end my life that way
I hear your cries of anger mom
I feel your tears of pain
And I know if your prayers were answered dad
You could hold me once again
So, please teach the children … teach them well
And guide them with your heart
They will know your wisdom comes with love
To keep them safe and smart
I was just 10 … **A Child Of God**
I would never be eleven
And to those I love … we will meet again
For my home is now in Heaven.

(This poem is dedicated to the hundreds of children who are abducted each year)

The Bells Ring Out

Christ was born in Bethlehem
And when he was just a boy
Began to preach God's words of love,
Of peace, goodwill and joy
His message spread
Throughout the world
To people young and old
For his words gave hope
To all who heard
And to this day, his story's told
So once a year
The world gives thanks
For his life upon this earth
And **The Bells Ring Out**
Each Christmas day
To celebrate his birth

Dancing Shadows

He sits there in silence
His button eyes stare empty at the door
As he contemplates
The sound of tiny footsteps as before
His body is now tattered
Aged with love through years of play
And the smile he smiles
Has never changed, not even to this day
When I was just a little girl
And nighttime came to call
It brought its scary shadows
That would dance upon my wall
But with my Tommy Teddy
Snuggled in my arms so tight
I knew that he would keep me safe
As we made it through each night
Coming home is special now
I've been away too long
I hold him once again and know
It's here that I belong
But now there is another child
Who holds my hand so tight
She too has **dancing shadows**
On her bedroom wall each night
She grabs for Tommy Teddy
With a smile upon her face
Though tattered, it's quite obvious
In her heart, he's won a place
She feels his love, it's plain to see
Even though she is so small
And I know Tommy Teddy will keep *her* safe
When shadows dance upon the wall

REASONS FOR WRITING EACH POEM

I'm Walking My Dog
This was an easy subject. Millions of people enjoy this daily ritual In fact, there's not a day goes by that I don't see *someone* walking their dog. I thought *"It's great in the good weather but what about winter !"* Well, that's another story here in Canada where the temperatures can dip way below zero. Like the poem says … "Just **who's** walking **who** in the snow?"

In The Rain
One day I was waiting for a friend to meet me at a local restaurant for lunch. Wouldn't you know it … it was raining "buckets". I was directed to a table that offered a street front window. As I was seated and anxiously awaiting my friend's arrival, I noticed an old vagrant man, struggling to walk down the street with his cane. He carried no umbrella and was soaking wet. I ran out and offered him my umbrella. He struggled to speak but managed to say *"thank you for caring"*.   Well, whoever and wherever you are …. this poem is for you.

Poofy The Duck
I was having coffee at one of my neighbour's homes one afternoon.   Just as I sat down, her young son came home from school crying. He told his mom he had been teased at school. She asked him what the problem was. *"Some older kids were laughing at my name."* he cried. *"I want a new name, mom."* he pleaded. Looking a bit frustrated she said … *"No, Aston, you'll just have to grin and bear it. It's a great name and they're just jealous!"*

"Hmm. A good subject for a poem" I thought.

Rags to Riches
Being positive in life and following your dreams is definitely something I applaud. After all, I'm sure we can all agree, it takes hard work and determination… many times against all odds. If you're a negative thinker, you'll probably never climb the ladder of success … at least not to the top.

Dad's Grandfather Clock
One of my aunts had a huge grandfather clock and when we would visit, she would often pull me into the living room to watch as it struck the top of the hour with such a thunderous "noise". It was a mystery why she did that. After all, you could hear that sound throughout her home and I often wondered if she ever got a good night's sleep !!

Seasons
We are so lucky to enjoy the 4 seasons here in Canada. This little poem was written to ac-knowledge that fact.

September 11th, 2001   (New York City)
After this tragic event happened, I tried and tried to write about it but very little ended up on paper. After a few weeks, I woke up one night out of a dream with what seemed like a good idea. At 2 a.m. I jumped out of bed and began writing as if someone was dictating the words to me. It took only a few minutes to complete. When I read it over coffee the next morning, I was satisfied with how it came together. Though simple in its presentation, it was exactly *what* I wanted to say and *how* I wanted to say it. I didn't change one word. I have since received a note of recognition for the poem from Rudy Giuliani who was the Mayor of New York City at the time of the attacks.

The Old Man By The Sea
On many beaches and landscapes throughout the world you will often run into an artist, trying to capture the beauty he sees and complete his vision on canvas for others to enjoy. This poem simply defines such a moment.

The Lottery
One of my friends simply suggested a title to me and dared me to write a poem about it. This is the result.

A Horse Called Jack
I suspect everyone loves horses. They are such majestic and beautiful animals. When I was 6 years old, I remember having my photo taken on a small pony. I cried the whole time ! I wasn't too brave when I was 6 years old, but, at Christmas I cried when they put me on Santa's knee too. What was I thinking !

A Cup Of Latte
Hmm. I wonder where I got the idea for this poem ! Sure... like many other people I meet friends all the time at coffee shops. It's just the thing to do these days. What's nicer than a good chat with someone over a cup of latte ! Besides that, I enjoy the personal touch rather than phone calls or the current technology. At least you get to talk face to face and hug them goodbye ... that's a good thing !

Numbers
This poem could have gone on forever as you can well imagine. An interesting subject though.

Here's To Marilyn Monroe
Marilyn Monroe was one movie star that kept the gossip columnists busy. It doesn't matter whether you were just a youngster or perhaps not even born at the time when she was making films, the fact is… she's still talked about today. A *"movie icon"* plain and simple. She definitely had *"charisma"* and *that's* something that cannot be taught. Either you have star quality or you don't and there's no denying the fact that our Miss Monroe certainly did !

Happy To Be Free
Ever watch tiny birds as they flit from branch to branch? They really don't stay in one place too long do they. Could it be they are wary of the larger birds and other animals that come their way? I love birds and couldn't write a poetry book without including them in one of my poems. For such tiny animals I can just imagine how much danger there is surrounding their everyday lives.

Today I Still Love You
The marriage of President Ronald Reagan and his wife, Nancy, was truly one of the great love affairs of our time but, as history has proven … all good things do come to an end. I had always admired both of them and was extremely sad when I heard that President Reagan was ill. Their love story was a catalyst for this poem. I simply wanted to acknowledge the fact that true love becomes even more precious as we grow old. This poem was included in "The Best Poems and Poets of 2003" and was placed on page 1. That book came out just days before his death.

Your Wedding Day
This poem was written for my daughter's wedding in 1998. That beautiful day will remain as one of my fondest memories.

The Rooster
The Rooster is a good luck symbol in some countries and a fun subject for a poem. Children get a kick out of putting in the rooster sounds with me as I read through it.

My Cherry Tree
When I was young, we had a huge cherry tree growing in our back yard. It was my job to pick up the cherries that fell to the ground and, believe me, it was quite a chore keeping up with that tree. Every day I would take my empty bucket out and every day would fill it with juicy sweet Bing cherries. What a treat ! I would often climb high up on a branch with a little cup of cherries for myself and enjoy eating them while watching the neighbours in their back yards. Mom was a fabulous Scottish cook and made the best cherry pies I've ever tasted !

You're No Tiger Woods
I must admit, golf has long been one of my favourite sports to play and to watch. Tiger Woods has long been one of my all-time favourite professional golfers and I try not to miss any of the tournaments he competes in. I couldn't resist including him in this poem.

Flowers
What person on this earth doesn't love flowers ! Every Monday and Friday, I prepare a fresh floral bouquet to place just inside the front entrance of my home. The beautiful scent of fresh flowers permeates the house and captures the feeling of being outdoors. To me, it brings back that old saying "stop and smell the roses". It really does make you feel good.

Whiskers
Now let's be honest ! Does lightning scare you ? Personally, I always hid in my closet when I was young and I always felt better when my little cat came with me. That way I couldn't **see** the lightning... even though I could certainly still **hear** it. I've actually met several people who've been struck by this force of nature so it's not as uncommon as some people may think.

The Flight Of John F. Kennedy, Jr.
I was invited to Washington, D.C. to attend a gathering of poets from all over the globe. The event happened shortly after John F. Kennedy, Jr.'s plane went down. I felt compelled to write a poem about this tragedy and did so on the flight to Washington. The opportunity came to read it in front of my peers and, to my surprise, received a standing ovation. Even though it is a rather short poem, it carried a big impact at that particular time.

The Camel
Through the years, I have found that children love to be read stories or poems about animals ... especially exotic animals. In this instance, it can be said that the Camel plays an extremely important role in long treks across the hot sands of his desert home.

My Fridge
"C'mon. A poem about a "fridge" you say?"

Well, when you think about it, it's one of the most important appliances in every household. It shouldn't be taken for granted ! Heck... when I was a young girl, I remember having huge blocks of ice delivered by the "ice man". In those days it was the only way we had of keeping our *"ice box"* (as we called it back then) cold. How could I possibly **not** write a poem about such a great invention !

I Still Smell The Roses
Memories of someone can be quickly revived by an old photograph, a scent, seeing a certain type of flower that they loved and, of course, countless other ways. There can be fulfillment, sadness, melancholy and certainly great joy in memories.

At The Zoo
I don't think there's a child in the world who doesn't love going to the Zoo to watch the exotic animals play. I always remember enjoying the antics of the little monkeys, the absolute beauty of the peacock and the giraffe so, of course, I had to include them in this poem.

The Good Life
Many of us have friends who, unfortunately, committed themselves to a relationship far too early in life, ended up getting married and even dropped out of school.   According to statistics, too few of these were lasting relationships and, more than not, end up in separation or divorce.   Marriage is hard enough *later in life* when the right person comes along and you have a solid and nurturing foundation to work with.   It's so true that women throughout the ages have been made to believe that the only purpose in life is to get married and have children ... which, for so many, means giving up their own goals and dreams.

My best advice came from my father (*and oddly enough as a poem*).

He said .... "Love can be fleeting but life is not.
So set your goals
Give it all you've got !"

This Mother's Wish
Self explanatory and a sad reality for many.

A Son's Prayer
Written for a special friend when his mother passed away.

The Snowman
Every once in a while I jot down a poem quite quickly, such as this one.   These, I like to leave for a week or two and then read again.   Many times I make changes but with this one I didn't. It turned out to be one of my favourites and I hope it becomes one of yours.

Winter's Perfect Moment
There's a lot to be said for summer fun but winter offers its special moments too. Especially here in Canada where winters can seem to last forever.   Yes, there is that perfect moment and one of them is sitting in front of the fireplace with a cup of hot chocolate, looking out at winter's newly fallen blanket of snow.   The chores have been done for the day, there are no buses to catch, friends to meet and, finally, the children are all snuggled in bed.
You are alone in the peace and beauty of winter's perfect moment.   Reflect and enjoy !

Candles All Aglow
Birthdays at any age are worth celebrating BUT when you get to your **85th**... well ... that's very special indeed. Never forget your loved ones on their birthday.   In fact, I've been known to get an un-birthday cake and gift for someone... *just because.*   Try it !   I guarantee it will bring the biggest smile to their face !

We Will Meet Again
I've had it mentioned that this comes across as a very spiritual poem.   As long as we have our memories, no one has truly left us.

A Man Of Vision

I had the pleasure of reading this poem a few years ago when I was in Washington, D.C.....
one short block from the White House.

My Dog Ralph

So many of us have fun loving, scruffy, lovable dogs like Ralph that mean the world to us. Yes,
they're there for us no matter what. When you think of it, few things in life compare with their
undying devotion.

Candlelight & Champagne

Hmm. What can I say about **this** poem ! I think I should stop while I'm ahead.

Every Moment

When someone asks … *"Why do you love me?"*… it's hard to put it down to just one thing.
Truth is, sometimes we don't even have the answer at that particular moment… at least one
that will be satisfactory. The fact is, our reasons for loving someone are ever changing. Life
can present new challenges and additional reasons for loving someone almost on a daily
basis ….and almost … *every moment.*

Mr. Snowy Owl

Do you remember *"show and tell"* days at school?

It was in my grade 3 class (*yes, I can remember that far back*) when a lady from the local
zoo brought in a Snowy Owl to show us. He was comfortably perched on her arm and she al-
lowed each student to come up individually and get a close look at him. He was absolutely
beautiful with his feathers of pure white and I remember how well behaved he was. He turned
his head and looked intently at each one of us as we came up to get a closer look. As long
as I live, I will never forget the experience.

A Child Of God

Yes, my poetry book is definitely diverse in its presentation of topics and I truly felt compelled
to include this poem.

Many years ago we lived a short distance from a family whose young daughter was ab-
ducted. Her body was found a few weeks later, not too far from where she lived. This was a
heinous act although certainly not an isolated case. Hundreds of children are abducted
each year and statistics suggest it most often happens close to home.

The Bells Ring Out

For years I've created Christmas cards to send to family and friends. This is one of the poems
from a selection of my cards that I thought I would include and share with you.

Dancing Shadows

I realized long ago that *treasures* are not always new or found within the vast array of "things"
on display in local or far away gift shops as we travel throughout life. A treasure can be a

memory ... or simply a long forgotten item from our childhood that brought us such great joy, warmth and happiness. In this poem, little Tommy Teddy is reborn. Found lost and forgotten amongst a little girl's childhood toys ... he is given a new life and loved once again.